VisualFestation

How I Manifested the Life of My Dreams & You CAN TOO!

PETER ADAMS

DEDICATION

This book is dedicated to my loving wife, Robin, for whom I am truly blessed and grateful to be lucky enough to have in my life.

CONTENTS

INTRODUCTION

First off I would like to say thank you for opening this book. I have read hundreds of great works from the ancient to the modern, and many are saying the same message just in different ways. Everyone has their own style of expressing things, and I will be doing that in my own way through this book.

What I have tried to accomplish in this book is to give you a simple overview of how I believe the Universe works. From there my goal is to help you define the life of your dreams. Lastly, I will give you the exact techniques which I have used and from which I have gotten amazing results in my life. I have used these techniques to work with the Universe and I feel as though my life is magical and truly blessed.

Everyone is in a different spot in their lives, and if you are reading this book, my guess is that you are looking for some type of change with something in your life. After reading this book, doing the exercises, and using the techniques you will have what you need to be, do, or have anything you want in this life. There is a disclaimer to that statement, and that is that you must believe beyond a shadow of a doubt that it is possible. To take that one step further, you are going to need to believe that it already exists for you and that it is on its way.

The concepts in this book which I have written about are universal, and they are true for everyone. I am not here to change anyone's belief system, challenge anyone's religion, or get into a debate about how the Universe was created. When I refer to the "Universe," it may be what you refer to as God, Buddha, Source Energy, Universal Life Force, or whatever you believe in. The important thing you need to remember is that whatever you choose to "call" it, it is still true.

If you are ready to start creating the life of your dreams, let us begin.

1 - TWELVE CRAZY GOALS

Time for a Change...

I, like many others, got introduced to the self-help industry as a result of being unhappy with the circumstances that existed in my life. I had been "downsized" as a result of a corporate consolidation, and I was unable to find a replacement job which paid anything near what I was formerly earning. Suddenly I clearly understood the meaning of a relatively new term known as "underemployed."

To make matters worse, I was working in a position that was not a spiritual match for my soul. My job duties as an analyst for a large for-profit hospital corporation included explaining why the hospital I oversaw had a good or bad month financially. What really bothered me was if we had a "good" month, that meant it was a tragic month for the patients and their families. It really hit home one day when I ran into a neighbor of mine in the cafeteria, who told me that his mother had been admitted and that she was not going to be coming home again.

The following month we had a "great" month financially, and I had to explain in my report that it was because we had an "outlier." An "outlier" in hospital lingo refers to a patient who has billed charges that exceed two hundred fifty thousand dollars ($250,000). Seeing my neighbor at the hospital and knowing that his mother's prolonged death was boosting our "bottom line," I knew I had to get out of this business. When it was bad it was good was not the kind of business I wanted to be in.

Being unhappy with my professional life, and simultaneously having financial challenges as a result of being downsized, I knew that I needed a major change. I don't remember how many times I could not sleep at night, and I would turn on the television to see Anthony Robbins' "infomercial" for his Personal Power System. I felt like he was really talking to me when he asked, "Are you ready to change your life? What are you waiting for?"

The only problem I had was that I didn't have enough money or room on my credit card to buy his system. Well, the Universe was not going to let money get in the way of getting Personal Power. The following morning, I ran into my friend Ron on the beach, and he told me that he had just bought it, and that he would let me borrow it as soon as he got through with it.

Now I was fired up, and I remembered Tony saying that we needed to take "massive action" on the infomercial. So rather than sit patiently and wait for Ron to finish the course, I got started immediately and went down to the local library and checked out a couple of self-help classics. One was the *The Power of Your Subconscious*

Mind by Dr. Joseph Murphy, and the other was *The Magic of Believing* by Claude Bristol. After reading these, it was clear that we could make massive changes in our lives for the better through the effective use of our subconscious mind.

Early one morning while sitting down on the beach, I meditated on the question, "What should I be doing with my life?" After a few minutes of meditating on that question, a "movie" started playing in my head. It was crystal clear, and it showed me being a real estate broker who was very active in charities, and there were pictures and thank you letters on the walls of my office. I don't know how long the vision lasted, but when I came out of meditation I had tears of joy in my eyes, and my body felt like it was "buzzing" from head to toe. Whatever this was, it was powerful, to say the least.

Over the next few days, I pondered over the idea that the Universe was telling me I should be a broker. Was that right? At the time I saw myself as a real estate investor, and Realtors were just people who got in the way of making good deals. I also had committed to opening a real estate investment company with a friend of mine who was moving to Florida, so I was going to make that my main priority. In the meantime, the "movie" got tucked away in storage, only to be recalled at a later date.

Ron finally finished going through Personal Power, and as promised he let me borrow it. I thought it was amazing, and I started incorporating a lot of what I heard on the audio CDs into my daily routine. One of the things I really liked was what Tony called an "hour of power." In his "hour of power," he talked about getting up in the morning and spending an hour alone and following a routine which consisted of exercise, meditation, and reading motivational material.

I made some tweaks to his program, and each morning after working out at the gym, I would drive down to the beach and spend sixty to ninety minutes on the beach doing my hour of power each morning before going to what I started to call my "temp job."

In my hour of power, I would get a cup of coffee at the local 7-Eleven and drive on to Siesta Key and down to Turtle Beach which was at the Southern end of the island. I would then grab my folding beach chair and a bag containing the books I was reading—a small copy of the New Testament, a notebook for brainstorming and scripting, my vision book, and my small notebook that contained my written goals.

One of the things I started to notice was the fact that if it rained out and I could not sit on the beach for my hour of power, I could feel the difference in my energy level and mood. I would actually feel like I was mildly depressed, which was not how I wanted to start my day.

One morning while driving to the beach, I was listening to Tony Robbins talk about traveling across Russia on a train, and during the whole trip he worked on setting goals, then rewriting them bigger and bigger until he was at a point where his goals seemed huge. When I arrived at the beach I decided that it was time for me to make some BIG goals which were going to stretch me out of my comfort zone. I took out a notebook and I started to work on goals which would cover business, health and fitness, travel, relationships, and my spiritual connection with the Universe. When I got done with the list, I had twelve goals written down which to me at that time seemed absolutely HUGE! I knew that if these goals came true I would have the life of my dreams!

The next thing I started to do was to work with my list of goals and try to develop what each one would "look" like, and what it would "feel" like when it manifested. I put a lot of thought into this, as I was serious about getting the results that I wanted. What I did next was to create a small notebook in which I included some affirmations, a few quotes from the Bible about prayer, and a list of my goals, and after each of the goals I drew a smiley face or two to represent happiness and gratitude for its coming in to my experience.

Goal One: "I AM HAPPY!!" ☺

The first goal was pretty straightforward, and it meant that I was happy with all aspects of my life. When I

7

would read this goal, I would get in to a deep feeling of gratitude for how great it was to be happy, and I would truly experience the feeling of being happy.

Goal Two: "**I have NO consumer debt!!**" ☺

The second goal was a real stretch for me at the time because I felt like I was being crushed by consumer debt. I had credit cards that ended up being maxed out as a result of me trying to subsidize my loss of income from the downsizing. I also still owed on student loans that helped me finance my undergraduate and graduate degrees. The payment on the student loans felt like a car payment for a Porsche that would never be paid off, and the minimum payment on the credit cards felt like a mortgage.

Between the credit cards and the student loans, I believe I owed roughly thirty-five thousand dollars. I wish that was all I owed, but it was not. We also had car payments; out of necessity we bought two new cars before the downsizing, as the ones we had were breaking down frequently with major repairs being needed. So add another twenty thousand dollars to the mix! Now we are up to roughly fifty-five thousand dollars in consumer debt and that didn't include our mortgage of one hundred thousand dollars. The one word which best described this feeling I had at the time was "hopeless." Well, Tony said think BIG, so I was taking his advice on this one.

To create the visualization for this goal, I would see myself going to the mailbox at the end of the driveway. When I got to the mailbox I would open it up to find it either empty, or just containing some junk mail. I would then "feel" how good it was to not have any bills in the mail.

At the time I set this goal, I got a sick feeling in my stomach every time I went to retrieve the mail in the mailbox, as it would be stuffed with bills, late notices, etc. If you are in a similar situation right now, let me tell you that it is not hopeless at all, and that miracles do happen. Read on.

Goal Three: "I am a very successful full-time real estate investor and self-made millionaire!" ☺

When I wrote this goal I was in the process of unwinding a real estate portfolio of ten rental homes which I had bought with my former business partner. He decided to move out of Florida, and we decided it was time to dissolve our real estate investment company. Creating the visualization for this particular goal was easy, as I was already in the business part time.

For this visualization I would see myself running through what my daily routine would consist of as a full-time real estate investor. I would see myself driving to the beach for my hour of power in a white Ford F-150 pickup truck with an extra cab and a tan interior. I would see myself grabbing my folding beach chair, my bag of books, and the daily newspaper to scour the classifieds for potential properties. I would also see myself going to a closing, shaking hands with the buyers, and picking up a check for the profits from a fix and flip.

One of the weirdest things that happened to me about 20 percent of the time that I tried to run this scene in my mind, was that instead of driving a white pickup truck, a pearl white Lexus LS 400 with gold package and chrome trim would "show up" in my visualization when I was trying to see the pickup truck. When this happened I would come out of my visualization and wonder why the heck a luxury car was coming in to my visualization. You can't haul Sheetrock in a Lexus, so how was I going to be a real estate investor? It didn't make any sense. The next day I would do the visualization again, and I would be happy to see my pickup truck back in my mind.

Goal Four: "I am fit and active" ☺

I would say "I am fit and active" more as an affirmation than something that I would visualize. At the time I had already completed three Ironman triathlons. An "iron" distance triathlon consists of a 2.4-mile swim, a 112-mile bike ride, and a 26.2-mile full marathon run. The training it takes to compete and successfully finish one of these is almost like having a second full-time job. So my goal was to maintain my fitness in the future.

Goal Five: **"We have newer vehicles owned outright"** ☺

This I would say as an affirmation, and I would feel how good it felt not to have any coupon books for car payments.

Goal Six: **"We have disposable money to have 'Real Vacations'"** ☺

At the time I wrote this affirmation, we were broke, and the only vacations we could afford were to take time off from work and have a "staycation" at home in Florida. For this visualization I would see us going on a ski trip to Colorado, and I would see my wife saying how much fun she was having, and I would have a feeling of gratitude that she was happy.

Goal Seven: **"I am able to give a lot of money to help others in need + Do!"** ☺

When I wrote this goal, I knew that I wanted to be a philanthropist. The reason I say that is that my wife and I had become active in Habitat for Humanity, which is a great cause. Habitat helps lower-income people afford a nice new home that they could not otherwise afford. The homeowners who get these homes pay for their "down payment" through sweat equity, which can often take them over a year to complete.

On one Saturday morning I asked the construction supervisor what types of appliances came with the finished homes. He said that they just came with a stove and a refrigerator. I told him that my wife and I were moving from a house to a condo and that we would not need our washer and dryer and would like to donate them if we could.

The supervisor said that "Mary" (not her real name) could really use them, as she was a single mother with four children. We had actually been working on her house together that morning. I walked over to her and said that I heard that this was going to be her house. She replied with, "Yes, isn't it just beautiful?" I then asked her if she could use a washer and dryer for her new house, and that we had a set that we didn't need.

I have a hard time describing what happened next. Mary screamed out "YES" in excitement and then hugged me. When she hugged me this amazing feeling of joy rushed through my body. It was if my whole body was buzzing. I had never felt anything like it before, but if this was what being charitable was like, I wanted to have this feeling all of the time.

To visualize this goal, I would see myself being at the ribbon cutting for a new home to be donated to a family by Habitat. I would see myself being called up to hand the scissors and the keys to the new family. I could feel that "feeling" I had from Mary's hug and I could see people clapping in joy for the new family. When I did this visualization I would always end up with tears of joy in my eyes.

Goal Eight: **"I live near the beach and have a beautiful home"** ☺

This I said as an affirmation, and I would have a feeling of gratitude for how happy I was to live near the beach.

Goal Nine: **"I own a large real estate portfolio"** ☺

I also said this as an affirmation to reinforce Goal #3 of being a full-time real estate investor.

Goal Ten: **"I am trusted by investors and have the ability to raise large sums of money"** ☺

At the time I wrote this I only had two investors, who were really close friends. I would say this as an affirmation with the feeling that this was absolutely true.

Goal Eleven: **"I have a great relationship with my wife"** ☺

I would say this as an affirmation and I would feel gratitude for having my wife Robin in my life.

Goal Twelve: **"I have a great spiritual relationship with God"** ☺

I said this as an affirmation, and I would feel gratitude for everything in my life for the things that were on their way.

What happened over the following three years of writing out these goals is nothing short of a miracle! Writing this down and realizing that this story happened to me inspires me even today. I was there and I still feel a sense of bewilderment as I relay the story and sequence of events which came to pass to make my dreams come true.

Without further ado, here's how it all played out on the Universe's playground. I got a notice in the mail saying that my real estate salesperson license was coming up for renewal and that I was required to take a mandatory continuing education class if I wanted to keep the license. I decided that it would make a lot more sense if I took a few extra hours and went for the real estate broker's license, and that way I could keep all the commission and could work independently.

It was at this point that I remembered the "movie" that had played out at the beach which had me being a real estate broker who was active in charities. Now that I was more spiritual I started to wonder if this was what I should have been doing before. I signed up for the classes and began working toward my Florida real estate broker's license. With my broker's license I could open up my own brokerage company. To adhere to the "movie" I decided that I would give 10 percent of our gross commission from each sale to charity.

On a Sunday afternoon in Sarasota in the spring of 2003, my wife and I were driving down to the waterfront to have lunch at a restaurant called Marina Jack. On the way I stopped at an ATM to get twenty dollars out. As we drove, we started throwing around names for the new charity-based brokerage I was going to open. We finally settled on the name "Benefactor Realty," and we went into the restaurant for lunch.

After lunch, we decided to walk along the waterfront park, which had a number of large sculptures on display.

As we walked down the sidewalk, a man came up to us and asked us if we could spare any money. He needed eight dollars so that he could sleep at the shelter and get a meal and a shower. I put my hand in my right front pocket and pulled out two dollars. I apologized to him for not having more, but he thanked us graciously.

As I walked away I remembered that I had gotten the twenty-dollar bill from the ATM and that it was in my back pocket. I turned around and went back to the man and saw that another Good Samaritan was handing him a five-dollar bill. Telling him that his luck was changing and now he was two for two, I gave him the twenty dollars I had found in my pocket.

There was something different about this person. He did not look like the many homeless I had seen before. He was dressed in the clothes of a tradesman, and he had the clearest blue eyes I had ever seen. As he started to walk along the waterfront with us he told us this story of how his girlfriend had hurt her back in a car accident and how she had gotten hooked on pain pills. He said that he had tried to take the pills away from her, and she had called the police on him and filed a restraining order saying that he was abusive. Now that he could not go back to his home, he was worried that he was going to become homeless.

To give him hope, I told him about the story of Og Mandino. Og was at one time in his life a homeless and hopeless alcoholic. Og started to read self-help books at the library and turned himself in to a millionaire, a bestselling author, and an incredible motivational speaker.

I also told the man that he should get his hands on a Bible. At that moment he reached into his pocket and pulled out a small brand new white-covered version of the New Testament. I don't know how I did this, but I went to look for the verse from the Gospel of Mark that I read every day on the beach, and as if by magic I hit the exact page on my first try. I read him the verse. I then went to find the verse from Matthew that I read in my hour of power, and AGAIN I hit the exact page on my first try. I read that verse to him and after telling him that everything was going to work out, I handed him back his copy of the New Testament. He thanked us again and said that we had really helped him out.

After I had walked about seven steps away from the man I got this "rush" of energy that I can only describe as what happens in that old television series *The Highlander*, when Duncan MacLeod goes through a "quickening." I could feel my whole body tingling the way it did the day Mary from Habitat hugged me. All I know is that whole experience was "strange," to say the least. I also remember wondering if that was somehow a test to see if I was serious about having a company called Benefactor Realty, and about giving to charity.

Not long after that, I opened up Benefactor Realty and began to work as a real estate broker part time when I was not at my temp job. Fortunately, most people who have jobs do most of their looking at properties on the weekend.

One Sunday afternoon, on our way back from looking at a restaurant site on the east coast, I received two calls saying that offers we had put in for a buyer had gotten accepted, which was great news, as we had another property go under contract on Saturday. I was now looking at making more money in three days than I could in six months on the temp job! My wife looked at me and said, "Pete, you can't afford to work there anymore."

We drove home and I wondered if I should really quit my day job and embark on this real estate thing. About ten years earlier I had tried leaving corporate to open a small business which didn't make it because it was undercapitalized, and I was worried about it happening again.

The following morning I went in to my office to try to figure out what to do. I will never forget the call that changed my life. It was around 10 a.m. on Monday morning when my office phone rang. It was my good friend Bill. I had worked with him and we had been downsized together by our former now bankrupt employer. When I answered Bill asked me, "What are you doing?" I thought this was weird, so I said, "Bill, you called me at work, what do you think I am doing?" Bill then said, "That's not what I meant. What I meant was, what are you thinking? Are you thinking about doing something?" I told him that I was thinking about leaving the hospital and selling real estate. He said, "THE MONEY IS THERE. THE MONEY IS THERE."

Bill then told me that he had been meditating at the lake by his house, when a message came beaming in from the Universe which said that he needed to call me and give me the message that "the money is there." You can't make this kind of stuff up. As if getting three deals under contract was not enough, now I had the Universe calling me on the telephone!

Not being one to question the Universe I immediately sent an email to my director to tell him I was going to be resigning. A few minutes later he called me to tell that he was happy for me, and that he knew it was only a matter of time before I left to do something with real estate.

I then went to meet with my original investors and asked them if they would be interested in investing with me again. This time it was going to be as a private line of credit for my new company. They were excited about the new opportunity and wrote me a check on the spot. Bill's words were now echoing again, and the money REALLY was there!

Driving back home on my normal route that week, I looked off to the side and saw a pearl white Lexus LS 400 with chrome trim and the gold package with a for sale sign on it. I pulled in to the parking lot and walked over to the car. It was THE CAR that had kept popping up in my visualizations. It was not a car that looked like the car, IT WAS THE EXACT CAR. Without hesitation, I called the number on the sign and bought the car.

I then got a call from a wonderful tenant we had in a rental property. She called to ask me if I would help her find a house to purchase, as she did not want to get priced out of the market. I said sure, and then I asked her if she wanted to buy the one she was in. She wasn't sure if she could afford it, but I told her I would help her with closing costs, etc. What I hadn't realized was that this property had appreciated by almost thirty-five thousand dollars over a two-year period since we bought it.

In less than a sixty-day period I had opened a new company and left my job, sold three properties as a broker, sold the rental house for a windfall profit, and paid off all my consumer debt, including the two cars, all the credit cards, and my student loans! This was totally out of the blue, and totally blew me away!

My life had completely changed for the better. When I wrote those dozen goals, I never saw any of this coming. I had no idea how it was going to happen; all I knew was that it was my job to keep believing it was going to happen and let the Universe handle the details. That same year my wife and I went on our ski vacation to Breckenridge, Colorado, and twelve months later we bought a waterfront home close to the beach. With help from the Universe we blew the "crazy" goals out of the water!

There was more to come the following year, and this is going to blow you away…

PETER ADAMS

2 - WINNING THE LOTTERY

After an unbelievable year during which all of my goals and dreams came true, I started to think about what else there was that I truly wanted to experience in my life. My life had become almost magical. It was clear that there was nothing that I could not be, do, or have if I practiced faith and used my visualization techniques. Being a triathlete, and having successfully completed five "iron" distance races, I started to contemplate the idea of racing in the Ironman World Championship in

Kailua Kona, Hawaii, which is often referred to as Ironman Hawaii or, as it is known in the triathlon world, "Kona." Anyone who has ever competed in an "iron" distance triathlon will tell you that being fortunate enough to compete in the Hawaii Ironman is like winning Wimbledon, the Masters, and the Super Bowl all in one day. Before I get into my next Ironman experience, let me give you some background behind the event.

The History Behind the Ironman Triathlon

The Ironman in Hawaii is a legendary race. It came in to being after a group of athletes were drinking beer at the Oahu Perimeter Relay post-race party in 1977. They were debating which type of athlete was the fittest. There was disagreement over who were the most "fit" athletes. Some said that cyclists were the most fit, others said runners were the most fit, and still others said that swimmers were the most fit.

To settle the score they decided to put it to the test, so they formed a new race that combined the three major endurance events they had on Oahu. They combined the

2.4-mile Waikiki Roughwater Swim, The 112-mile Around-Oahu Bike Race, and, to top it off, they added the 26.2-mile Honolulu Marathon course. They deemed that the winner of this race would earn the title of "Ironman."

The first "Ironman" triathlon was held in 1978. There were fifteen brave and also crazy participants who competed in the first race. The really remarkable thing about it was that they did not know if anyone could possibly finish the race. No one up to this point had tried to swim 2.4 miles, then cycle 112 miles, and wrap it up with a full 26.2-mile marathon. There was no "cut off" time to any of the events, and the finishers would receive a handmade "ironman" statue made out of metal with a cast iron nut for a head. They felt that a nut was symbolic for the fact that they had to be "nuts" to try to do this. Twelve of the original fifteen which started the race received the statue, which is absolutely amazing to say the least.

In 1982 the race was moved from Oahu to the more rural "Big Island" of Hawaii. Today there are a number of "Ironman" races around the world, and it is a global brand and business. Every athlete who has ever competed in an "iron" distance triathlon owes a great deal of thanks to these pioneers of the sport.

Back to my story...

In the early Ironman Hawaii races, you could simply pay a fee and get in to the race. Now there are a number of Ironman triathlon races around the world, and the Hawaii race is the world championship for the series. Essentially every triathlete in the world dreams of competing in this race. Unfortunately, now you need to be one of the fastest triathletes in the world, or you need to be one of the luckiest to win a spot at the starting line.

Not being one of the fastest in the world meant that if I was going to get in to Kona, I was going to have to be one of the lottery winners. Each year the WTC (World Triathlon Corporation), who owns the rights to the race, holds a lottery whereby 200 people out of over 10,000 entries are allowed into the race, and they post the results on April 15.

After thinking about the race for about a month, and with the deadline rapidly approaching to enter, I decided to really put my beliefs to the test. I got out my credit card and put my name "into the hat" for the 2005 Ironman World Championship lottery. As a member of the St. Pete Mad Dogs triathlon club, I knew a ton of people who entered their names in the lottery for "Kona" multiple times who have never gotten in. I knew that if I wanted different results, I was going to need to do something that they were not doing. The difference was visualization.

Having watched the video coverage of the race that year in 2004, which had amazing coverage of the course, I decided to buy the DVD and watch it repeatedly. With less than four months before the winners of the lottery were chosen, I knew I had to get serious. I started watching the DVD a few times a week, and I would mentally race the Hawaii Ironman in my mind for around twenty minutes each morning.

The DVD had great footage, and the way they filmed it, you truly felt as if you were watching it as a competitor. Some of the most memorable shots were of the swim start, where you saw the competitors' feet kicking underwater directly in front of you, and you heard the narrator say, "You are in Hawaii, and you are in the Ironman." Another one I really liked showed the race leader biking in the lava fields on the "Queen K," with the shadow of the helicopter which is filming him caught on tape as they passed over him. This was very helpful for creating extremely lucid visualizations.

I also found a picture in the back of an issue of *Triathlete Magazine* which was entitled "Night Moves." The picture showed some taller triathletes walking in the dark on the "Queen K," and a shorter, stocky triathlete running up behind them. The caption says, "As night slips over the last remnants of a very long day, triathletes continue toward the finish line at the Ironman Triathlon World Championship in Hawaii." I cut the picture out and put it in my vision book. I am stocky and typically pass a lot of people in the dark when I race. That man in the picture now was me, and I visualized the scene more times than I can count.

Before I knew it, it was time for the lottery results to be announced. I went over to my friend Bryan's office to meet him for lunch. His secretary said that he stepped out to get a hair cut and that he would be back shortly. I looked down at my watch, and suddenly I realized that it was just about noon, and it was APRIL 15! LOTTERY TIME...oh my gosh I was nervous...I sat down behind Bryan's desk and hopped on his computer to look up the results on the Internet.

I could not believe my eyes. The very first name on the list was "Pete Adams FL." Was that me? Was there another Pete Adams? The hairs all over my body stood up, and I couldn't believe it had happened. Bryan walked in the door about ten seconds after I saw my name on the list. I said, "Check this out" and pointed to the web page. He thought I was playing a practical joke on him, and that I made up a fake list. Suddenly my cell phone started ringing off the hook with numerous triathlete friends calling to ask me if I knew that I got in to Hawaii! He then said, "Holy shit, dude, that's awesome!"

Bryan was my training partner for a number of Ironmans that we raced together, and he knew what a once in a lifetime thing this was. We were both stunned with amazement, and we kept repeating how we couldn't believe it had actually happened. I called my wife to tell her the news and she could not believe it either. I remember her saying, "No way...Are you serious?...Oh my God, Pete, that's AWESOME," and then her cell phone started to ring with friends calling to tell her the news.

I cannot tell you the amount of gratitude I felt when I heard the news. The Universe had done it AGAIN! WOW!

"You Are in Hawaii and You Are in the Ironman"

Six months later, and just like in the video, there I was standing in the body marking line carrying my transition bags and getting the number "813" stamped on my body. If you have ever done a triathlon, right before the start of the race, your nerves and emotions are in overdrive. Kick that up about a thousand percent, and that is what this race feels like.

After body marking, we headed over to drop off my bags and I did a final check on my bike to make sure the tires weren't flat. Now it felt like a mini eternity as I treaded water and waited for the start of the race.

The cannon went off, and the swim portion of the race was on. As I swam I could see the feet kicking in front of me and I heard the narrator's voice in my head saying, "You are in Hawaii and you are in the Ironman." It was just like I was in the 2004 DVD—I mean REALLY like I was in the DVD. I seriously started to wonder if I was really here...really in Hawaii...really in the Ironman, or if this was a dream I was having that just happened to be VERY real.

The swim is my weakest event, so after emerging from the Pacific I didn't have a hard time finding my bike, as there were very few left in transition. I hopped on my bike and the adrenaline really kicked in, as there were people everywhere cheering us on. In town there is a loop at the beginning of the bike course, and I passed my wife and friends who were cheering me on two times before leaving town. After passing them at "hot corner" for the final time, I rode up Palani Road and then out to the lava fields on the "Queen K" highway.

Out on the Queen K and heading out past the airport, I finally settled down and got into a good rhythm on the bike. It was very desolate in the lava fields, and again it looked just like the DVD. You have plenty of time to think on a 112-mile bike ride, and I again started to wonder if I was REALLY here or not. I started to wonder if I might actually be dead, and God was letting me do the race as part of Heaven. I am not joking when I say this. I even started to wonder if I was in a cycling accident, and maybe I was in a coma or something.

In this race, drafting on the bike is not allowed. So when you pass someone, they are supposed to fall back and keep a three-bike-length gap between racers. About 35 miles into the bike course, I found myself in a section of the course that had a series of rolling hills. I was taking turns passing and being passed by a female racer on a green Griffen tri bike. She was lighter than me, so she typically passed me on the climbs, and being heavier I passed her on the descents.

This went on for about ten minutes, and then I rode up next to her and she looked over at me. I asked her point blank, "Are we really here?" Her response was, "Yeah, I know what you mean. It's surreal." At least I was not the only person having these thoughts. I felt better but I still wondered if it was a dream.

I started to make my way up to the turnaround at the town of Hawi (pronounced "Hahvee"), and the winds were getting really strong. It was a serious crosswind, but at the time I confused it for a headwind and started to look forward to the tailwind I was going to have on the way out of town.

After stopping at the bike special needs station and eating my Ironman racing meal of choice (boiled ham and white cheddar cheese on white bread with yellow mustard), I hopped back on the bike to make my return ride back to Kona.

Heading out of Hawi, I realized there was no tailwind waiting for me. Instead, it was headwind part II. I was now pedaling my brains out and only going 17 mph downhill! I should have been going around 40 mph down a hill like this. Now I was starting to worry about making the bike time cut off.

I finally made it back to Queen K and back to the lava fields. When I was making the turn I saw a racer who had a different style bike hydration system; it looked more like a tank. He hadn't hit the winds on the climb to Hawi yet, and I felt sorry for him. All I could think was that I was glad that I was not that "poor bastard."

I didn't know it at the time, but his name was Jon Blais and he was known as the "Blazeman." He was out here doing the Ironman while suffering from an incredible pain from a deadly, advanced stage of incurable ALS, more commonly known as Lou Gehrig's Disease. He had a special hydration system because he could not catch bottles at the aid stations, as the disease had taken away his ability to grab and hold things. Jon was a spokesman for ALS, and was an amazing human being. Jon made it to the finish line that day in Kona; unfortunately, a few years later that horrible disease took his life.

Heading back through the lava fields, all I could think about was how much easier it was on the way out. As I rode I could hear a helicopter getting closer, and before I knew it it was above me and the shadow of it passed directly over me and my bike. It was EXACTLY the way it happened in the 2004 DVD; the only difference was that I was not the race leader. The "shadow" thing freaked me out and now I was almost convinced that I was not "here."

After more wind and many more miles of lava fields I finally got back to town. The first person that I recognized in hours was my wife, who was cheering me on from the road below the Kona Brewing Company. It was so good to see her, and she was cheering me on and saying, "Looking good!" For a moment the pain in my back, neck, legs, and buttocks temporarily lessened, and I headed down to T-2 to put on my running shoes and start running the marathon.

I rolled out of transition and headed up to "hot corner," where my wife and friends were cheering me on like I was going to win this thing. I actually felt pretty good, and I shook off my "bike legs" in just a few miles. I took a couple of turns and ran up Alii Drive going past Island Lava Java, which was absolutely packed with cheering fans. The view of the surf crashing across from Lava Java was absolutely AWESOME, and I felt much gratitude and gave thanks to God for letting me be in Hawaii and do the Ironman.

After a few more miles I saw Sarah Reinertsen running toward me. She was like a rock star out here, complete with her own van with a film crew. Everyone knew her name and went crazy. For those of you who don't know who Sarah is, she was a lead story in the 2004 Ironman DVD. Sarah is a challenged athlete, who as a child had a tissue disease and had to have her leg amputated above the knee when she was very young. In 2004, she attempted to be the first above the knee amputee finisher of the Hawaii Ironman. If you watch her story in the 2004 DVD, you had better have some Kleenex handy because it is a real tearjerker.

In the 2004 race, Sarah didn't make the bike time cut off and was not allowed to continue on. In 2005, she was back in the race with a fitted bike from Trek, with the words "Unfinished Business" painted on the frame. When Sarah and I passed for the first time, I knew that she was going to make it this time. She was running strong and she had a smile on that made everyone around her feel good. Sarah knew she had this one in the bag, so it was time for her to enjoy her journey.

I finally caught up with Sarah and made the pass. I really didn't want to pass her because I was having way too much fun being near her and basking in her glory. When the people cheered for Sarah, you just felt good to be near her, and it took your mind off of the pain. It was almost like a contact high. If she could be out here doing this grueling event on one good leg, you had better not start feeling sorry for yourself.

After heading out of town and watching a beautiful sunset over the Pacific, I started out toward the airport and the infamous "energy lab." At this time of day the "energy lab" was not viciously hot, which it is famous for when the pros come through. On the way out I got to see Sarah again; she was pretty hard to miss with the film crew chasing her with mikes and spotlights in hand.

Now it was really dark out and I remembered the photo from *Triathlete Magazine* that I cut out and put in my vision book. I was really the guy in the picture now, as I was running up on the other racers who were walking. Now all I wanted to do was to get back to town, before I got in a wreck with some overzealous fan on a mountain bike.

The course now was pitch black with the exception of the aid stations, which had lights powered by gas generators. All I had to do was to keep running to the next set of lights, where I would be greeted by the nicest volunteers in the world, and I would make it "home." The mantra now was just keep moving. Just keep moving.

I finally made it out of the darkness and reached the outskirts of town and back to civilization. With every step I could hear the announcer and the cheering crowd get louder and louder. I ran down Palani and through "hot corner" and took a left. Now I was running parallel to where the finish line was and I was close but not there yet. My everything ached with every step of that run on the final few miles back to Alii Drive.

As I got closer I remembered the advice that a friend of mine gave me when he heard that I got in to Kona. He had done the race a few years before, and he said,

"Whatever you do, don't race hard down the finishing chute. Take your time and enjoy it. You will never forget it as long as you live. Trust me."

The last two miles felt as long as the previous twenty-four. *Where was the turn?* I kept thinking. Finally I saw a police officer blocking traffic and I knew that was where it was. *It is about time,* I thought, and I turned right and ran downhill on to Alii Drive.

What was to happen next was one of the most memorable things that has ever happened to me. I was running down Alii Drive and there were children and adults from the crowd running up to me and high-fiving me. They wanted to share in this incredible moment, and it felt absolutely AMAZING to have them there! I finally arrived at the entrance to the finishing chute, and I could see the finishing line in sight.

I have been to a lot of races, but I have never seen anything like this! People were jammed in the bleachers screaming and cheering. The finishing chute had people lined up shoulder to shoulder on both sides screaming and banging noisemakers. There was so much energy here that you probably could have lit up a city with it. It is something you have to experience in person to appreciate.

I took my time and ran down the final steps of the chute and crossed over the finish line. I don't have words to describe what that was like. It was almost like you never wanted that moment to be over, even though you spent the entire day wishing it would be.

After crossing the finish line I was given a fresh lei of flowers which smelled amazing, a towel, and my Official Finishers Medal. A moment later I was greeted by Robin and friends at the finish line who wanted to help me out in any manner possible. I told them I was all set, and that all I wanted was to head up to the hotel room so that I could drink a cold beer and take a hot shower.

As I made my way through the crowds of spectators, everyone I passed said great job or congratulations, and all I could do was say thank you. Thank you to all the fans. Thank you to all the volunteers. Thank you to the original fifteen racers from 1978. Thank you to my wife and friends for their great love and support. Thank you to the race gods of the Big Island for watching over me. Thank you, Lord, for this amazing experience which I will always remember with great joy and gratitude!

As they say in the Ironman world, "Anything is possible." I hope this story has made you a believer of the same.

3 - THE VISION HOUSE

In the spring of 2004, my wife, Robin, and I watched a story on the Travel Channel on Breckenridge, Colorado. I had written in one of my journals one morning on the beach that one of my goals was a ski vacation in Breckenridge under my "places to travel" list.

A few months later, I was talking to my new friend Doc, whom I met through a real estate course, who had lived in Colorado. I mentioned that I wanted to check out Breckenridge, as I had seen a special on TV. Doc said that he had a timeshare in "Breck" and that we could use it, as they didn't think they would get out there that year.

I went home that evening and told Robin about it... suddenly, I ran out to the trunk of my car and found the notebook from the beach and showed it to Robin. "We are enjoying our ski trip to Breckenridge." The hairs were standing up on my arms. IT WAS WORKING AGAIN. We ended up not taking the timeshare but instead booked the week we wanted before Christmas. ("We are now having "real" vacations!")

We went back out to Breckenridge for vacation again in December of 2006. One morning on our way out to go snowmobiling, we drove past a subdivision that had beautiful log mansions overlooking the Ten Mile Range. After snowmobiling, we decided to drive through the subdivision to take a look at the homes.

By now we understood the power of visualization, and I knew I wanted some new "material" for my vision board and vision book. We drove around the subdivision until we found the house we thought had the best view. We took a picture of the house, along with a picture of the view it had. After arriving home I had a friend of mine print them off in color, and I put the two pictures in my vision book.

These pictures to me represented my "ideal scene," because if we lived in a house like this as our second home, we obviously were very successful. What I would visualize was that I would be having conference calls with our asset managers, and after these meetings I took the afternoon off to either go skiing or play golf, depending on the season. Many times if I found myself unable to sleep, this was the visualization I would use to burn into my subconscious mind before falling back to sleep.

I probably did this visualization over 500 times. In the summer of 2010, we decided to escape the Florida heat and work remotely from Breckenridge, Colorado. We found a very small furnished cabin to rent off of Craigslist that was only about a mile from the subdivision where we took the pictures in 2006. That summer we rode our mountain bikes through the subdivision and took more pictures. We really loved that summer out in Colorado, so we decided to look for an annual rental.

After going to a yoga class on one Friday afternoon in July, Robin returned home to search the Internet for an annual rental. After an hour or so of searching various Web sites and not finding what she was looking for, I suggested that she check out Craigslist. On the second page of ads she found a home that sounded very interesting. She started looking at the pictures and she said, "Pete, you have got to see this house!" I walked over to where she was working on her computer, and when I looked at the pictures, I realized it was THE HOUSE in my vision book.

The hairs on my arms stood up when I saw the pictures. I was in complete amazement. I asked Robin who the contact person was for the ad. She told me the name, and for some reason I knew I had heard the name before.

I did a search on the name in my email, and I found the name connected to an ad off Craigslist for a garage apartment I had inquired about back in March of 2009. I asked the owner if she could send me some pictures of the apartment. She did, and once again, the hairs went up on my arms when I looked at a picture taken out of a window, and the view was almost identical to the one I had in my vision book. Now I realized that my "vision house" had came in not once, but twice!

I replied to the email from March 2009, and we called the owner and set up a meeting with her on the following morning to see the home. She gave us the physical address, and we drove by the property a few minutes later because we could not wait to see if it was the same one. Five minutes later, we knew beyond any shadow of a doubt that it was the SAME HOUSE as in my vision book. We couldn't believe what was actually happening.

The next morning we drove back over to meet with the owner and to get a tour of the house. The owner was very nice and we spent ninety minutes meeting with her over coffee learning about their beautiful home.

I don't know if I can describe the feeling of total awe and amazement that was going through my mind and body as we toured the house. Looking out the windows and seeing the same view I had been "seeing" in my visualizations was almost overwhelming. We talked with the owner regarding what a strange "coincidence" it was for us finding each other twice off of Craigslist in two different years on two different ads.

We didn't mention the pictures from 2006, the vision board, or the visualizations of doing conference calls with the asset managers, etc. We were worried that she would think we were delusional and had stopped taking our medication or something! We told her that we were interested and asked her to send us an application.

We then drove off to go mountain biking in Colorado Springs, and the rest of the day we kept asking ourselves whether or not that had really "happened." It was so unbelievable that it was almost too much to comprehend. It proved that creative visualization worked; I mean REALLY worked. These experiences were manifested, and it had nothing to do with fate or coincidences, or whatever.

We all have the power to create the life and circumstances in our lives which we desire. I hope that you have found my experiences to be an inspiration to you.

4 - QUANTUM PHYSICS & ENERGY

Quantum physics is a very complicated subject, and I honestly cannot say that I am an expert on the topic. Rather than make this a technical discussion on quantum theory, I prefer to simplify it for you.

In short, everything in our Universe, when broken down into the smallest building blocks, is one thing, and that is energy. Everything you see, feel, taste, etc., is composed entirely of energy. You may never have thought of this before, but you are also comprised of energy. If you looked at your body through a very powerful microscope, you would see that at the smallest level, you are in fact energy.

To take it one step further, your spirit or soul, whichever feels more comfortable to you, is also energy. In this case it is Divine energy.

Is it a "wave" or a "particle"?

Quantum physics is the study of subatomic particles, the smallest building blocks of matter, and how they react. One of the most fascinating things that scientists discovered is that when they measured subatomic "particles," depending on the test performed, the result was that the particle could be either a "particle" or a "wave." It was actually a probability amplitude, whereby it was simultaneously both a particle and a wave.

If that wasn't strange enough, they then did further experiments and concluded the "observer" affected the outcome of the experiment just through observation.

The truly amazing thing this proved was that the researcher's thoughts were affecting the outcome of the experiments. Thus, thoughts were actually real things which had the energy to shape the outcome. What this told us was that the entire Universe is made of this "energy," and that outcomes could be manipulated by our thoughts.

At this energy level we are connected to Source Energy, which is also the level of creation in the Universe.

5 - IT IS ALL IN YOUR MIND

Your thoughts are things, and they are creative in nature. Unfortunately, almost everyone in the world does not realize that they share in the creation of their own life through the thoughts that they think. Many people believe that they live in a predetermined life that is guided by "fate," and that they are just along for the ride. Nothing could be further from the truth.

To make it a little clearer, imagine that you are both the Leading Character, as well as the Screen Writer, in the movie called *Your Life*. The script is written by the thoughts you think, which then attract the "scenes" in your personal movie called *Your Life*. If you don't presently like the way the "scene" *Your*

Life is playing, rewrite the script to change the "scene." Most Screen Writers unfortunately suffer from "writer's block" when it comes to writing the next scene. As the Screen Writer, you can create any movie of *Your Life* as long as you believe that you can.

"G.I.G.O."

"G.I.G.O." is an acronym that stands for "Garbage In, Garbage Out." Let's bring this in to the realm of thought. If you think negative thoughts on an ongoing basis, you are going to see negative outcomes happening in your life. It is not by chance but instead by natural law.

One of the most damaging things that our minds can do if we are not vigilant in watching over our thoughts is to create what I call the "downward spiral." In the "downward spiral," thoughts of fear generate more and more thoughts of fear and in your mind things are getting worse and worse. It is almost a total "fear fest" that is being choreographed completely in your mind as a result of "wrong" thoughts.

"Downward Spiral" Example:

An example of this could be a salesperson who is worried about making his or her quota. The salesperson starts to think ideas like this:

-If I don't make my quota, they are going to fire me and I won't have a job.

-If I lose my job, then I won't be able to find another one.

-When I can't find another job I am going to lose the house.

-When I lose the house I will lose my family and no one will love me anymore.

-I will then be homeless and die from "fill in the blank" all alone...

Now the movie escalates into a full-blown tragedy, and the salesperson is *feeling* as if this "reality" is actually happening. The stress of these negative thoughts could then translate into lost sales due to reduced effectiveness from insomnia. The problem with these "spirals" is that they get out of control and will eat you alive with real stress. If these thoughts are not cancelled out, they can become a self-fulfilling prophecy through negative outcomes being attracted to your life experience.

Whenever your mind starts trying to play the "spiral," you immediately need to forcefully say "STOP!" You are the one who is in CONTROL of what you are going to think, and it is not going to be things like that! Period.

Remember that nothing good can ever come from thinking negative thoughts, so decide now to purge them from your being.

Thought Barriers & Misguided Beliefs

It is not my intent to give everyone a prepackaged excuse as to why they are not living the life of their dreams through what I am going to say next. The truth is, from the time you were born to where you are right now, you have been subjected to "brainwashing." This "brainwashing" took place when you did not even realize it was happening. It could have been positive, but more than likely you received negative reinforcement.

Most likely, the greatest amount of "brainwashing" you received came from your parents, and the "brainwashing" continued to be administrated by relatives, friends, community, religion, formal education, etc. You were bombarded with negative misinformation, which you became convinced was the "truth," as it was being told to you by your parents, who "knew everything." Right?

Unfortunately, young minds are easily poisoned from the misguided beliefs of a person they love. The greatest tragedy is that these false beliefs continue to exist at some level in your mind.

The most common example I hear on a regular basis is: "I can't (be, have, or do) what I truly want because of _____."

Question: How do you know that if you have never tried?

Answer: "I just know I can't because of _____."

Now that you are older, it is time for you to drop the limiting beliefs that are in your head as a result of your life up until now. If your parents, or whoever, instilled in you the belief that you cannot do, be, or have something, drop those beliefs NOW!

Another common flawed belief many people have is that somehow they are not "worthy" of having the life of their dreams. Where did that idea come from? It is not serving you, so drop the idea that you are not immediately! You ARE worthy! You were sent in to this experience to live the life of your dreams and were given free will to attain it.

Limiting beliefs oftentimes are so strong that they keep people from even trying. What have you told yourself in the past that you could not do? Be honest. We have all done this many times in the past. The past is the past, so let's drop this mental "baggage" that has been weighing you down for so many years, and move on. The sooner you do this, the sooner your life is going to get better.

You are working with a Universe of infinite possibilities and infinite resources. You are not living in a world of lack, or limited resources. That may be how it appears to you on the physical plane, but that is not the truth. The truth is, the more you have, the more there is. The Universe is constantly expanding, and everyone can have everything they want, if they believe they can and if they are willing to do their part.

What Should I Be Thinking?

That is a good question, and the answer is straightforward. You should be thinking about what you want in your life, and not worrying about what you don't want in your life. I am sure you have heard the common phrase "when it rains, it pours." What you may not have realized is that it a time-tested example of the Law of Attraction in action.

As an example, let's say your automobile breaks down, resulting in an expensive repair at the garage. After you pay the mechanic, you hop back in your car and all you can think about is how "broke" you now are...ten minutes later your cell phone rings, and it is your spouse calling to tell you the air conditioner stopped working...with dread you start to worry about how you are going to afford to pay for it....you then realize the traffic ahead of you has stopped, and you notice too late and plow into the back of the car in front of you, badly damaging both of your vehicles. The next day your boss asks you why you need an advance on your paycheck, and you respond with, "You know what they say; when it rains, it pours."

What you think about and focus on is going to show up, so you need to be sure that what you are thinking about is a match to what you want to manifest in your life. If it is more money that you want, you need to get in to the "feeling" that you already have plenty and are blessed with abundance. If this is the first time you have heard this, it might sound delusional, but it is not.

The "feeling" in this case is a vibration that is being sent through your thoughts out to the Universe. A mismatch in vibration will be corrected over time by the Universe. In this case it may be the temporary appearance of a money shortage. If you refuse to "buy in" to the appearance and hold steadfast to your belief by "feeling" that you have plenty, the Universe will bring the circumstances needed to match your vibration.

The Universe can do this in an infinite number of ways, one of which might be you suddenly land a huge client for your business, or "out of the blue" you receive a check from Uncle Bob who just sold his company for $10 million and is feeling generous, or a "million dollar" idea comes to you about an invention you were working on.

To people on the outside, this will just look like "luck." There is no such thing as good luck or bad luck; there is such a thing as positive or negative expectations. These expectations that you have, whether positive or negative, will attract either good circumstances, or bad circumstances, which will show up in your life.

We are going to go through some exercises in Chapter 8 that will help you define what it is that you say you really want. Once we have defined it, we can then build upon that to create the techniques we will use later in the book.

6 - FEELINGS & GRATITUDE

Simply put, like attracts like. So you need to do a really good job of monitoring the thoughts you are currently thinking, as they will lead you to a state of feeling either good or bad.

Think of your feelings as an early warning system to what you are thinking. If you feel bad about something, and continue focusing on it, you are going to amplify that bad feeling. Through amplifying that bad feeling, you are going to attract into your life more of what will make you feel bad. That is absolutely not going to be a favorable thing for you when you get more and more things to feel lousy about.

One of the best examples I have heard about the Law of Attraction is this. Imagine that the Universe is a giant mail order company, and the way that you place your orders is through the thoughts you are thinking. On the other side, imagine that there is a shipping clerk filling your order. The shipping clerk does not know if size 8 will fit you; all the clerk knows is that is what you ordered. Therefore, it must be the size you wanted.

Sometimes these orders get shipped to us with "bonus extras," which could be really good, or really bad, for that matter based on what we are thinking. The good thing about all of the orders we place is that they can be cancelled before they are shipped, through a change in our thinking.

The best thoughts by far that we should be thinking are thoughts that give us a feeling of gratitude. Through feeling gratitude, we are telling the Universe thank you. When we feel gratitude we are connecting directly to Source Energy through love, which is the most powerful force in our Universe.

When you express a true feeling of gratitude to the Universe, you are doing a lot more than giving thanks for your current blessings. You are also setting the stage for more good things to be brought in to your time/space experience, so that you have more and more to be grateful for.

When you express gratitude for the things that have not yet shown up in your experience, that is even more powerful, as you have now taken a goal or an intention and converted it into a form of prayer. One of my favorite passages from the Bible that addresses this is from the book of Mark 11: 23-24, when Jesus says:

"For verily I say unto you, That whosoever shall say unto this mountain. Be thou removed, and be thou cast into the sea; and shall not doubt in his heart, but shall believe that those things which he saith shall come to pass; he shall have whatsoever he

saith. Therefore I say unto you. What things soever ye desire, when ye pray, believe that ye receive them, and ye shall receive them."

That is one of the most powerful statements ever told about how to create whatever it is that you wish to experience. Jesus is telling us point blank HOW to create miracles in our lives. Many people equate the word "miracle" to something that is incredibly large, such as taking a few fish and a couple of loaves of bread and feeding thousands of people.

That is not what I am saying at all. A miracle could be that you are in a terrible car accident and walk away from it without a scratch. Another could be that a medical lab test comes back negative, or that money from an unexpected source shows up precisely when you need it. These are all miracles, just on a smaller scale than, say, parting the Red Sea.

The process I described above as giving thanks and having gratitude for the miracles that have yet to appear in your life puts these miracles in motion.

One of the biggest things we need to address here is that you don't get caught up the "hows." You don't need to know "how" the miracle will manifest; all you need to do is believe that it will and be grateful for it now.

If you start thinking or worrying about "how" it is going to happen, or what if it doesn't happen, you are "watering down" your faith that it will, and you are providing resistance to the event manifesting in your experience. The "hows" are to be left to the Universe to solve, not you. The Universe connects all the circumstances that lead to the fulfillment of your miracle, so stay out of the way and let the Universe do its job. By the way, you are going to love the results!

7 - "ASK AND IT IS GIVEN"
...AND YOUR ROLE AS A "CO-CREATOR"

There have been numerous books (this one included), and recently a movie, all about the Law of Attraction and the process of creation. "Ask, believe, and receive" was told to us over two thousand years ago by Jesus and was recorded in the Bible in the book of Mathew 7: 7-8:

"Ask and it shall be given you; seek and ye shall find; knock, and it shall opened up unto you: For every one that asketh receiveth; and he that seeketh findeth; and to him that knocketh it shall be opened."

A question that you may want to ask yourself is why, after all this time, do we still not get "it"? My personal belief is that a lot of people have been told by various religions that somehow "God" is separate from them, that they are not worthy, and if you don't follow our dogma you are going the spend the rest of your days in a hot place and they don't call it Florida.

In fact, nothing could be further from the truth. There is a piece of the "Creator" inside you, and you do have the power to create miracles in your life. I wrote this book to convey that message to you and to share the techniques I have used successfully to create the miracles in my life.

One of the things I think most books fail to get across is that you need to take action. This is what I define as the "Co-Creator" piece. In your role as "Co-Creator," there are a number of job duties that come with the position, such as the following:

-Decide what it is that you want, why you want it, and be able to create desire for it.

-Believe that you do have the power within you to create anything!

-You need to get into the "feeling" of already having it.

-You need to have gratitude and believe that it is already on its way to you.

-You need to avoid anyone who says that for whatever reason you cannot be, do, or have what it is that you say you want.

-You need to practice the techniques I am going to share with you on a daily basis until you receive what it is that you want.

-If there is something you need as a skill to do whatever you say you want, you need to take specific action and acquire those skills.

-You need to make a permanent commitment to remove procrastination from your life.

-You need to stay out of the "hows" and leave that job up to the Universe. The Universe reorders itself to make your miracles come true; you don't need to know "how."

-You need to develop the skill of endurance, as this is a lifelong journey, and there will be times when you may doubt that everything is working.

If you fulfill your duties as "Co-Creator," you will have whatever it is that you say you want. The Universe will see to it.

8 - DEFINING YOUR DREAM LIFE

Three Not So Simple Questions

Ask yourself:

"What would I be if there was nothing that I could not be?"

"What would I do if there was nothing that I could not do?"

"What would I have if there was nothing that I could not have?"

These are not philosophical questions. These are very important, very deep, and very personal questions. These are not questions that you can answer quickly, unless you have already been asked and answered them before. The answers to these questions will tell you what you really should be doing with your life.

This is no time to be thinking small, so I want you to come up with answers to these questions that are so HUGE that if they happened, you would be so completely blown away beyond your wildest dreams! When you are working on the answers to these questions, don't let your mind say things to you like "You can't do that," or "You'll never have that." Your mind is just talking "trash," so tell it to be quiet.

The "Whys"

Take your time answering these questions and feel free to "super size" your order. If you can imagine it, you can have it. Once you have your major life goals written down, I want you to write each one down on the top of a separate piece of paper. Below that I want you to write out all the reasons "why" this goal is so important to you, and next to each of these reasons, I want you to write out the "feeling" you have associated with this reason.

Your feelings are the real underlying reasons why you want to achieve these goals. This is a good thing, because if you dig down deep enough you will find that the answer in its simplest form is Love. With Love comes passion, and that is a very powerful force of attraction in our Universe.

"Ideal Scene"

Once you have your list completed, I want you to take a few minutes and imagine that it is now five years in the future, and everything on your list came perfectly true, and that it IS now your present reality. See yourself in the "movie" that is playing on the screen of your mind with all of these things being true.

When you are ready, grab a notebook and write out precisely in detail what this scene looks like and how it feels—I mean really *feels*—to you. Soak up all those awesome feelings associated with these things being true in your experience. Does that feel great or what?

Congratulations, you have just defined your "ideal scene," which is also known as your "end result." Now you not only have a destination for your journey, but you already know what it is going to "feel" like when you get there. Now that you have this, it is time for you to learn the techniques which will bring your "ideal scene" in to your reality, along with all those good feelings that come with it!

9 - GOAL SETTING

The importance of having goals cannot be overstated on the journey to living the life of your dreams. When I talk about goals, I am not referring to New Year's resolutions, where people resolve to lose weight and they go to the gym for two weeks!

I like to think about goals as being similar to mile markers on the road to your destination. In this case, that destination is your ideal scene, or your dream life. One of the best things about setting and achieving your goals is that it puts you in as an active participant in creating whatever it is that you say you want. If you want to have the life of your dreams, you are going to need to take action.

Dreams with Deadlines

Another way to think about goals is to think about them as being dreams with deadlines. Many people are actually afraid of setting goals, as they immediately start to have thoughts such as, "What if it doesn't happen, and how bad will I feel then?" If this sounds familiar to you, you are going to need to make those feelings about goals to be something that is now in your past.

Another error many people make is that they will set a goal, but they fail to set a date for its achievement. "When I am ready" is not a deadline; it is a delay tactic for avoiding taking the actions required. Let's say your goal is to "one day" complete that college degree that you started but never finished for whatever reason.

The first thing you need to do is to drop that "one day" nonsense and set a deadline for achieving that degree. You also will need to take immediate action such as ordering your transcripts, filling out the application, and registering for classes. As soon as you do this, you are moving in the direction of your dreams and achieving your goals along the way.

Deeds, Not Words

I have an excellent example of this from my personal experience which I would like to share with you. In December of 1988, I was a construction worker in the Laborers Union working in Boston on an excavation site. The weather this particular day was lousy, half raining and half snowing at the same time.

I was in my twenties, and I was working with another Laborer who was in his fifties. The two of us were shoveling gravel with yellow rain gear on, and it was pure misery. The gravel was wet and heavy and by the morning coffee break, my lower back was already hurting. After the short break it was back to the "rock pile" to try to survive until lunch.

I will never forget this day as long as I live. We were taking turns shoveling the gravel when suddenly I looked up in horror and realized that I was looking at myself in thirty years! It hit me like a sledgehammer! What the hell am I doing? I've got to do something about this and I've got to do it NOW! The rest of the day I worked on my action plan while I shoveled away. It was time to go back to school.

I had attended a community college briefly four years earlier and left before the end of the semester to go make "big bucks" in construction. I decided to take the next day off from work so that I could visit the college and see if they would let me back in. They said no problem and gave me an application and the spring course catalog.

I then called one of my friends to get the number of one of his friends who was a shift manager at a hazardous waste plant to see if there were any night openings. My timing could not have been better. He said he was looking for a couple of people and hired me on the spot.

That spring I started taking classes part time as a freshman at the community college. At the same time one of my friends was a first semester junior doing a cooperative learning assignment at a stock brokerage firm. Five years later I earned my bachelor's degree, and two years after that I had my master of science degree.

After seven years, my friend was still only a junior and talking about taking classes to complete his degree, and I had graduated twice. The major difference was that I took immediate action, instead of just sitting around talking about it. When you make the commitment and take action, the Universe will bend over backwards to help you achieve your goals.

Words, Not Thoughts

Your goals need to be written, and you need to review them on a daily basis. Simply put, if they aren't written, you don't have them. Writing them down forces you to define clearly what it is you are going for. For your subconscious mind to assist you with achieving these goals, they need to be clear. Through writing them down, you are able to give your subconscious mind clear instructions.

I personally suggest having a laminated card which you can carry in your pocket at all times so that your goals are with you at all times. What I found helpful and which added "power" to my goals is that I added some short prayers to the opposite side. Another technique that I have used in the past is to rewrite my goals every morning. When you do this, it feels as if you are reinforcing your commitment to their achievement.

Can You Believe Them?

Your goals also need to be believable to you. Don't confuse this with the idea of knowing how they are going to come to fruition. That is not what I am saying. What I am saying, though, is if you create a really big goal, one which is beyond what you can get your mind to believe can happen, it is too big for you at this time. What will happen is that you won't be able to achieve the *feeling* that it has come true.

As you set goals and achieve them, you are going to gain momentum and set bigger and bigger goals. One of the ways you can work on ramping up the size of your goals is to work on your faith. If you can truly believe with utmost certainty that your goals are already accomplished, you can pretty much ask for anything because you will be unstoppable.

The "Why" Is as Important as the "What"

When you create your goals, make sure you know why you want to achieve them. The reasons why you want to achieve these goals need to be powerful. If they are not powerful you will not be able to generate a burning desire to have them fulfilled, which is necessary.

This burning desire is also known as passion. If you don't have passion for what it is that you say you want, simply put, it won't happen because the energy is not there. With passion for their fulfillment you will be able to generate very strong feelings of gratitude for their coming into your experience ahead of time. This is a crucial step in the process of manifestation.

In the Present...

Lastly, when you write out your goals, you must write them in the present tense. What I mean by that is when you write them down, write them as if they have already manifested.

Let's say one of your goals is to finish college. You would write that goal down as "I am a college graduate," rather than "I am going to finish my degree." The difference between the two statements may seem subtle, but it is huge. The first one puts it in the present as already being done, while the latter places it as a possibility in the future.

All of your goals need to be written in the "now," and as already being a reality. Doing it this way, you will be able to generate the belief and the feeling of gratitude for it already being done.

10 - VISION BOOKS & BOARDS

If you have read the earlier chapters of this book, I am sure you are going to be interested in what I have to say about vision boards and books. My personal experience has been nothing short of miraculous, when I look back to what I have put in my vision book, and which HAS manifested into my reality.

In case this is your first exposure to vision boards and books, I will give you a quick explanation on how to create one. I will then tell you how I used one to successfully help me manifest things into my physical reality.

Let's Create One...

The first thing you need to do is to create the list of goals for which you have passion. Once you have done this, the next step is to gather pictures of what the attainment of these goals "looks" like.

As an example, let's say your goal is to take your family on a vacation to Disney World. What you could do, then, is to get some marketing brochures from Disney, which are filled with photos of families having a great time at the park, and cut out the pictures of the families having fun. More than one picture is preferable, as it will give you more "material" to work with. Once you have these photos, you can fasten them to either a book or board, or both.

Take your time doing this and make sure you find the best pictures you can. Remember, this is your life we are talking about, and "okay" is not going to cut it. So make sure you find pictures that you can look at and generate the feeling of truly having what the picture represents to you.

Where faith and belief is such a crucial part of the manifestation process, I highly recommend finding some spiritual verses that resonate with you and adding them in as well.

In my vision book, I have some powerful verses from the Bible which I typed on my computer and printed out. I then inserted them into transparent sleeves and then placed them in a three-ring binder. What I found to work best with me was to alternate the pages of verses with the pages of the pictures. Feel free to customize your book to what works for you.

Inside your book you will also have your written goals, which must be written in the present tense. One really good way to do this is to write them as affirmations or as "I am..." statements. Let's assume that you are single and your goal is to be in a loving relationship. You could write your goal out as "I am so happy to be in a loving relationship."

The important thing to stress again is that the statement must give you the ability to have the "feeling" that it is true. Below that statement you could have a picture of a smiling couple who look to be having a wonderful time together.

When you are done, your vision book should look like a representation of the life of your dreams! As the "pictures" in your book become your actual reality, and I promise you they will, move those pages to the back of your book. That way, when you see them in the future it will thoroughly reinforce the fact that you are a "Co-Creator" and that you have the power to manifest things into your reality.

Now that you have created your vision book it is time to use it. The vision book is really a tool for you to use to create the feeling of already having the life of your dreams. At this stage you have already defined what it is that you want to have in your life. You know why you want it and you have true passion for it showing up in your life. Having pictures of what it looks like now is very powerful.

I cannot explain to you exactly how it works; all I can tell you is that when you combine this with visualization, you are going to be blown away by the results!

PETER ADAMS

11 - CREATIVE VISUALIZATION & MANIFESTATION

Before I get into how massively powerful I believe the process of visualization is for manifestation, let me first explain to you what I am talking about. The process of visualization is to actively use your imagination to create the "movie" in your mind of what your dream life looks and truly feels like. When done effectively, you will be able to create a visualization which will seem as real to you as the dreams you experience when you sleep.

I am going to go through the techniques I practice, and if you want to learn more I suggest reading an excellent book entitled *Creative Visualization* by Shakti Gawain. I learned the "Pink Bubble" technique, which I will discuss later, straight from Shakti's book.

The Visualization Process Step by Step

One of the things you must be able to master to have really good visualizations is the ability to quiet your mind through meditation. If you are new to meditation, don't worry, you are not going to have to get on a plane to Tibet to learn. It is a lot simpler than you might think, but I would suggest reading more on the subject.

To begin, you need to be able to relax, turn off your "outside" thoughts, and bring your brainwaves down to a state known as "alpha." At alpha, you are completely relaxed, but you are still awake. Alpha can best be described as the state which you are in just before you fall asleep. At that level you are very relaxed but you can still control your thoughts.

One of the techniques I use to get into alpha is to sit in a comfortable chair, close my eyes and relax, and then count backwards from fifteen to one. I actually see the numbers, and I relax more and more as I count down. Finally at one, I arrive at alpha and I am completely relaxed.

Once you are at alpha, you can begin your visualization process. When I first started to practice visualization I would get into alpha and imagine a beam of white light passing through my body from the heavens to the center of the Earth, and it would flow in and out with each breath, and after a handful of breaths I would feel a sense of connection with the Universe.

Once I was at this level I would begin my visualization process, which would last between five and ten minutes, and I would step in to my "dream life" or "ideal scene" where all of my goals had manifested. An important note I would like to add here is that when you are in your "ideal scene," you are not visualizing about "how" it is to come about; instead, you are enjoying being in the "end result."

One of the most important things you must have when visualizing is the ability to generate the *feeling* of joy and love that it has come true, and to bask in that good feeling. We live in a feeling Universe, and these good feelings you experience are going to attract more experiences for you to have good feelings about. Eventually, these good feelings will be accompanied by the actual manifestation of the "end result" into your reality that you are now visualizing.

Before you come out of your meditation, imagine the "ideal scene" now surrounded by a pink bubble, and get into a feeling of total joy and gratitude to the Universe for bringing this to you. The next thing to do is to "see" the pink bubble float higher and higher, getting smaller and smaller as it rises to the heavens and eventually disappears. Now slowly open your eyes and realize that you have done your part, and the Universe will bring it to you. Know and feel this to be true without any doubt.

In the "pink bubble" technique just described above, the color pink is associated with "love," which is the most powerful force in the Universe. The "bubble" floating to the heavens represents "detachment" from the outcome, whereby you are not worried about it coming true, because you know that it IS true.

My Personal Successes

I personally cannot tell you how truly powerful I believe the power of creative visualization to be. My personal belief is that when we are practicing the techniques, we are truly operating as "Co-Creators" with the Universe and operating in the field of infinite possibilities where anything and everything can be created.

There is going to be a time delay between practicing your visualization exercises and when the "things" you want to show up in your reality arrive. If you were someone who could operate at the vibration level of a "Christ" or Buddha, the time delay would be much shorter. The most important thing you need to do is **believe with faith** that it is done and on its way to you and that it is only a matter of time before it shows up.

The coolest thing is when it does show up you will never see it coming ahead of time. When you look back, though, sometimes you will be able to "connect the dots."

A great example of this is when what appear to be "challenges" in our lives show up. Sometimes the "challenges" are precisely part of the Universe's plan and they are actually events needed to "create" the circumstances for our dreams to manifest. We don't realize this because we are not able to "peek behind the curtain" to see how it is all actually happening.

Don't become disappointed by mistaking "challenges" as anything other than everything working out perfectly. When your dreams manifest, and they will, you will see that it was all part of a master plan to get you where you say you wanted to be, do, or have.

Acting as a "Co-Creator" and through using creative visualization, I have and continue to manifest miracles in my life. If you regularly practice visualization, the miracles that show up will be yours, and is that going to feel good or what?

I do need to make you aware of something before we close this chapter. Sometimes, for whatever reason, you are going to have days where you seem unable to get into the "zone" and will have difficulty visualizing. On an occasional basis this happens to me as well.

Don't worry about it. When this does happen, and it will, just work on one of the other techniques such as scripting, which we will discuss in the next chapter. This will keep you on track and focused on your path to the life of your dreams!

PETER ADAMS

12 - SCRIPTING

Scripting, which is sometimes referred to as "journaling," is a great technique I use regularly to get in to the *feeling* that my dreams have manifested. It is a really easy exercise to do, and it is great when you are pressed for time.

There is something very powerful about writing words down on paper. It is especially powerful when you are writing them down while simultaneously having a feeling of gratitude. It only takes a few minutes, and you can generate some amazing feelings of truly having it now.

It is important that you find a quiet place to write without distractions. From there break out your paper and pencil, and start writing about the miracles that you want to have materialize in your life, and the associated feelings of joy and gratitude now that they have become your reality. You should be able to generate the same level of feelings when you are scripting as you do when you are having a good day visualizing. What I normally do is start off with a statement such as "I am so happy about _____ ," and then I start writing about and describing how "good" it feels to have _____ in my reality.

Sometimes I will focus on practice scripting on one of my goals; other times I will script for a longer period of time and write about my entire "ideal scene" and the feelings of joy I have for it manifesting into my life. Don't worry about your penmanship or spelling when you are doing this exercise; what is more important is that you can get into the flow and just let the words and feelings come out. Never feel as if you are forcing the words to come out, and never think or write about "how" it is coming to you. Remember, you are writing in the present tense, and it has already happened.

A Brief Example

Let's say one of your goals is to have a cabin in the mountains. Here's how I might write about it...

"Wow!! I cannot believe how much I love spending time at our new cabin next to the lake! I love meditating next to the crystal clear pristine waters every morning. I feel so at peace here. The kids are having such a great time swimming that I can barely get them to come out of the water to eat. The sunsets over the lake are absolutely beautiful, and I love the cool evenings here. Lord, I cannot thank you enough for my beautiful cabin. I love being here so much that I never want to leave. Thank you! Thank you! Thank you!"

If you have done this exercise correctly, when you are done writing you should really be basking in a feeling of joy and gratitude.

Another method of scripting is to imagine that you are writing a letter to a very close friend or loved one and you are telling them all about the miracles that have happened to you. The more detailed you can be about your feelings and the experience, the better. You can use scripting to improve any area of your life that you wish to change. One of the things that I do when I am scripting is to add the "pink bubble" visualization technique when I am done writing, thereby releasing it to the Universe to manifest it back to my reality.

13 - AFFIRMATIONS

Affirmations are powerful statements that you repeatedly say aloud back to yourself. The idea behind them is to put your subconscious mind to work on bringing these affirmations into your reality. The affirmations are always written or said in the present tense and they are always positive. Your subconscious mind does not recognize the words "no" and "not," so do not use them when you create your affirmations.

Let's say one of your goals is to lose 50 pounds and to get back down to your ideal fit bodyweight of 130 pounds. Rather than creating an affirmation that says, "I am no longer fat," a better way would be the following affirmation: "I feel great maintaining my perfect weight of 130." Some people have had great experiences with saying their affirmations while staring at themselves in the mirror.

The technique which resonated best with me was to add the specific language to my affirmations. At the beginning I would add the words "In an easy and relaxed manner, in a healthy and positive way, I am now...(then state my affirmation)" and then I would close with, "In its own perfect time, for the highest good of all concerned. This or something better is now manifesting on my behalf." I have to credit Marc Allen for this technique, which I learned from reading his book *The Millionaire Course.*

Example: One of my actual Affirmations

"In an easy and relaxed manner, in a healthy and positive way I am now building financial success which is beyond my wildest dreams. In its own perfect time, for the highest good of all concerned, this or something better is now manifesting on my behalf."

This was one of the affirmations I created back during the time I was working on my Twelve "Crazy" Goals. In closing, I think the best method to practice affirmations is to create one for each of your goals, and then to repeat them when you first rise, and again just before sleep. Then visualize and see them as all being true in your mind before drifting off to sleep.

PETER ADAMS

14 - AS IF...

Think, speak, and act "as if" is a technique whereby you get in to the mindset and feeling of "being," "having," and "doing." What you are doing is creating a state of mind in which you feel as if you have already achieved your goals, and you create these feelings ahead of the actual event.

You also combine this with action and do the things you will do when your dream life manifests, as well as acquiring the knowledge that you will need to be ready when your goals show up.

One of the things you may need to get over is the concept of "make believe" as something only children play. You live in a world that is "make believe," and never forget it. Wherever you are in life right now is a result of what you have "believed" and "made."

Now that you have been told this, it is time for you to use this knowledge to your advantage. Think of this as being similar to your visualizations, except that now you are doing them and you are fully conscious. To better get this concept across, let me give you an example from my life.

"The Color of Money"

A few years after I bought that white Lexus LS 400, which I wrote about earlier in the book, I found myself wanting the newer model Lexus LS 430. I put a lot of miles on the LS 400, and I loved the car, but it was starting to wear out after I put about 180,000 miles on the odometer. One of the things I liked best about the newer LS 430 was that they added a wood insert into the steering wheel and dashboard which really dressed up the interior.

Knowing the power of being a "Co-Creator," I drove down to the local Lexus dealer and picked up one of their sales brochures, which had a bunch of great pictures of both the exterior and interior of the car. I then cut out the best picture of the car and put it in my "vision book," and I put the brochure in my "hour of power" bag which I brought to the beach each day.

After a while I really "knew" what my "new" car looked like. When I would walk off the beach and get back to the LS 400, I would imagine that I was opening the trunk of my LS 430, and I would get into the feeling of how great it felt to have this beautiful car with a fantastic interior. Another thing I would do is to visualize and "see" in my mind's eye the wood accent interior of the LS 430 while driving the LS 400. This technique worked best when I would drive in the early morning before sunrise.

Another thing I would do to get ready for the LS 430 was research on various Internet sites to figure out what the true market value was for each year. I would then "shop" for LS 430s on eBay Motors, and I would look at all the pictures that the sellers posted on their ads. When I saw one that I liked, I would take it one step further and plug the information into another site, which would give me a valuation based on the year, options, and mileage.

I really liked my LS 400, as it had reached out and "found" me, so I felt loyalty to her. One morning I hopped in the car to drive to an appointment to show a house to a client, and the car was completely dead. After messing around with it for ten minutes, and covered in sweat from the sweltering Florida summer, I finally started the car and made it to my appointment.

When I got home after the showing appointment, I went directly to eBay Motors and found a "deal" on a beautiful dark green LS 430 nearby, and I clicked the "Buy It Now" button. After a few days I appropriately named the car "The Color of Money."

The feeling I had now when physically driving the LS 430 was exactly the same as the "as if" feeling I created when driving the LS 400. Now in the morning when I came off of the beach I was "really" putting my beach chair and bag into an LS 430. All I could do was smile and feel gratitude, which is precisely how I prepared for this day through practicing "as if."

Whatever it is that you want, make sure that you do your "homework" to prepare yourself. Then practice the feeling of "as if" for HAVING it now, and feel real gratitude, for it is just a matter of time before it manifests into your reality.

15 - PUTTING IT ALL TOGETHER

These techniques that I have described to you in this book are the exact ones I used successfully to manifest miracles in my life. If you want to manifest the life of your dreams, you now have all the tools to do just that. Feel free to use them in combination, or as stand-alone techniques. Over time you might want to change them around so that you stay focused and fresh. The most important thing that makes these techniques work is your faith and belief that they are already "done" and on their way.

I hope that the miracles which I have manifested successfully using these techniques have made you in to a "believer" in the fact that you are a "Co-Creator" and that you have the ability to truly create the life of your dreams. I hope that you will share this knowledge with everyone that you love, as they too deserve to live the life of their dreams. We are all here to help each other, and imagine the joy you will feel when they tell you that you have totally changed their lives.

I have given you all the knowledge and the tools you will need to be, do, or have whatever it is that you want. It is now up to you to take action. I wish you Godspeed on your journey.

All the best!

Pete

ABOUT THE AUTHOR

Pete Adams is a philanthropist and both a Master and Teacher of the Law of Attraction and Manifestation. Pete has studied the greatest teachers of all time, and he has combined their teachings with specific techniques which he has successfully used to create miracles in his life.

Since 2004, Pete has been a full-time entrepreneur and business owner in various aspects of real estate and finance. As an Author & Teacher, he now feels that it is time to share his techniques and message with others to greatly improve the quality and satisfaction of their lives.

Pete proudly served his country as a paratrooper in a United States Army Long Range Surveillance Detachment (LRSD). His interests include: reading, golf, tennis, skiing, hiking, snowshoeing and competing in endurance athletic events. He is a seven-time finisher of the Ironman triathlon, which consists of a 2.4 mile swim, a 112 mile bike, and a 26.2 mile run. In October 2005 as racer #813, Pete competed and proudly finished the Ironman World Championship in Kailua-Kona Hawaii.

Pete and his Wife Robin have been happily married for over 24 years, and they spend their time enjoying a very active and full life between Florida, Colorado, and Hawaii.

Made in the USA
Monee, IL
21 May 2022

96841535R00080